THE BRIDGE

BOOKS BY HART CRANE IN
LIVERIGHT EDITIONS

The Bridge

White Buildings

The Complete Poems & Selected
Letters & Prose

THE
BRIDGE

A Poem by
HART CRANE

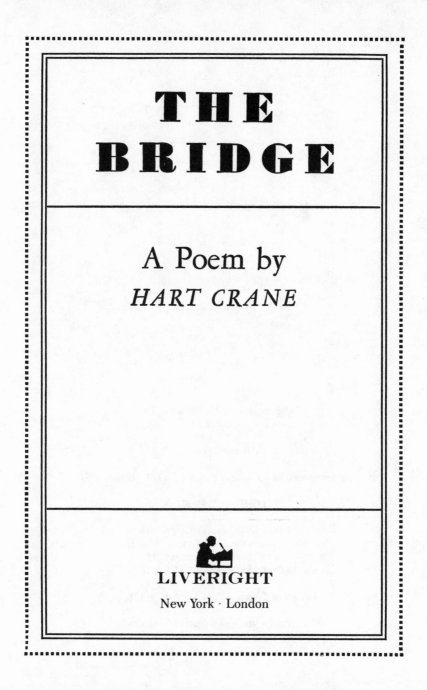

LIVERIGHT

New York · London

First published as a Liveright paperback 1970; reissued 1992.

ISBN 0–87140–225–4

Liveright Publishing Corporation
500 Fifth Avenue, New York, N. Y. 10110
W. W. Norton & Company Ltd
10 Coptic Street, London WC1A 1PU

Library of Congress Card Number 79–131276

Printed in the United States of America

1   2   3   4   5   6   7   8   9   0

From going to and fro in the earth,

and from walking up and down in it.

THE BOOK OF JOB

CONTENTS

INTRODUCTION

I_T is strange for me to be adding a note to the introductory comments of Waldo Frank, which were my own introduction to *The Bridge* more than ten years ago. After living with Crane during those years, reading several thousand pages of commentary on him and his work, and adding my own to the growing pile, I find that Frank is still an excellent starting point for a comprehensive view of Crane's poetry and its place in modern life and literature. Like all commentary, it tells us at least as much about the critic and his time as it does about the poet; for, like all great poets, Crane has proven to be bigger and better than any single view can account for. In my brief remarks here I shall risk being assertive, as Frank was in 1932.

Without attempting to refute his general sense of *The Bridge,* I would like to identify a dimension of the poem which Frank was unable to deal with, but which must be the starting point for the contemporary reader. In one sense, this is our gain. But what we can't see—and this says as much for us in our time as it does about the poem—is the "message" of optimistic regeneration that Frank confidently predicted we would be able to take for granted, the message that would be "too obvious . . . for general interest." Frank approaches the poem looking for "a conscious, substantiated theme or principle of vision to stratify the interacting parts of the poem into an immobile whole." The conscious theme of *The Bridge* in this sense is an obvious one; it is the note of ecstatic affirmation sounding in the final section, the *Atlantis.* But that section of the poem was the first part which

Crane actually wrote. The rest of the poem was composed during five agonized years of struggle and creativity, in an attempt to *reach* the envisioned end. To pass over or dismiss as flaws the agony and doubt in the poem, and to accept as an expression of faith what was primarily an attempt to achieve faith in the vision, is to polarize the possible responses to the poem—to make it merely an echo of our own optimism if we happen to be so blessed, or to make it poetic rant if we are skeptically inclined.

If, however, one approaches *The Bridge* without a precommitment to finding a final answer, it is possible to find in it a theme or principle of unity which speaks to the widest range of the human and artistic predicament. This theme may roughly be described as a quest for a mythic vision, rather than the fixed, symbolic expression of a vision firmly held in the poet's mind. The vision sought is one that will assure a hopeful future in the face of a sorry present; one that will be based on an intuition of a glorious past, and provide a bridge from that past to the hoped-for future in spite of the present. The poem is highly subjective in language and content, and understandably so, because the quest is a personal quest, the search of the poet for a vision that will satisfy his own needs. But like his Romantic predecessors, especially Blake whom he admired above most poets, Crane saw the problem of the poet as reflecting the central problem of the society in which he lived, and the poet's solution to the problem—if he could achieve one—as having consequences far beyond the poet's private life.

It is a terrific problem that faces the poet today—a world that is so in transition from a decayed culture toward a reorganization of human evaluations that there are few common terms, general denominators of speech that are solid enough or that ring with any vibration of spiritual conviction. The great mythologies of the past (including the Church) are deprived of enough facade to even launch good raillery against. Yet much of their traditions are operative still—in millions of chance combinations of related and unrelated detail, psychological references, figures of speech, precepts, etc. These are all a part of our common experience and the *terms,* at least partially, of that very experience when it defines or extends itself.*

Against the background of the daily cycle from Brooklyn to Manhattan and back, essentially a closed and discouraging routine, the poet carries on his quest, ranging into the legendary aspects of the past for elements still viable in the present, and for signs of hope on which to base an affirmative attitude toward the future. It is not by accident that rainbow images appear throughout the poem; for Noah's voyage to the future, after God's flood had destroyed all evil in the present, symbolized for Crane both the harsh omnipotence and the benignity of some greater force controlling destiny. The rainbow is thus a visual image for a concretely perceived—though symbolic—bridge, and a symbol of hope for men who are beset by present peril. The quotation from *Job* on the title page is not a casual reference, for Crane saw himself, like Job, suffering the agonies of doubt and despair, attempting to nourish a faith that could finally be confirmed only by the Word of a voice out of the whirlwind. It is Satan who comes to God, "From going to and fro in the earth, And from walking up and down in it," and Crane is like Satan too, tempting himself on to the verge of re-

---

* From "General Aims and Theories," included as an appendix in Philip Horton's *Hart Crane* (N.Y., 1937) p. 34.

nouncing his vision yet hoping that the vision, like Job's prayer, is pure.

If we look at the poem alert to the poet's need for constant self-assurance in his quest, we can see an ambivalence in it which enriches its significance for us. In Part Three, *Cutty Sark,* the parade of clipper ships is not simply asserted as one more bit of evidence foretelling the new Atlantis. The poet is at the end of his day; the nickel playing the juke box has run out; the dawn is putting out the Statue of Liberty. He starts to walk home across the bridge, but he can't complete the trip because he has still not found the Word he must bring back. Instead, he turns to a catalogue of clipper ships which were glorious in their time but are now gone. The ominous, defeated tone here makes it hard to see how "the poet is out again, now seaward," unless he is moving seaward to be lost in time with the *Rainbow* and *Leander* and the other glories which are "no more." Similarly in Part Four, *Cape Hatteras,* Crane distinguishes between Whitman as the blithe Saunterer on the Open Road, and the Whitman who lived through the tragedy of the Civil War. It is the latter who may enable him to see "Easters of speeding light" in the airplane's plunge to destruction, linking World War I with the Civil War in the line of grim realities that must be faced before a true affirmation can be reached.

The final crisis of the poem comes in *The Tunnel,* with the apparition of Poe gazing back at the poet in the reflection of his own face in the subway window. It is the subway that "yawns the quickest promise home," that focuses all the horror of the modern world into a psychic hell through which the poet must pass, like Aeneas and Dante before him, before he can find the Western Path. Poe is not the technological prophet who foresaw the method for fulfilling Whitman's vision, he is the test-case. In these "interborough fissures of the mind" he replaces Whitman as an index of the poet's experience, and Crane finds in the agony of Poe's last night a closer analogue for his own emotional state.

> And when they dragged your retching flesh,
> Your trembling hands that night through Baltimore—
> That last night on the ballot rounds, did you
> Shaking, did you deny the ticket, Poe?

The poet hovers on the verge of losing his faith completely and wonders—for he can never know—if Poe lost his faith under comparably agonizing circumstances. What must be born, before the poet can speak his word of faith to the world, is his own private suffering. And he must bear it without the crutch of poetic convention or the "subscription praise" of orthodox religion. This is the poem's most intensely personal moment and yet, like the final moment of Christ's agony, it may be seen as the poet's taking on himself the burden of our collective psychic ills without any assurance of a resurrection.

When the poem finally reaches its conclusion in the *Atlantis,* we must be able to hear in the midst of the "Psalm of Cathay" the tone of doubt that gives it a desperate urgency rather than a triumphant finality. "Hold thy floating singer late!" he pleads, as if conscious that this vision he is trying to sustain is in danger of disappearing once more into the teeming span. *Is* it Cathay, he asks in the final stanza, that the "orphic strings" sing? As Orpheus lost Eurydice when he turned to look at her, the poet may lose this vision

INTRODUCTION

after the poetic ecstasy of expression passes. The "arching strands of song," the "humming spars" and "chimes," do in fact give way, when faced with the question, to ambiguous and undecipherable whispers. The poet ends with a confession that he can never know whether or not "a god" is "issue of the strings."

Crane constantly referred to himself, while writing the poem, as being "in the middle of *The Bridge*," and at one point he noted that his poem, like the physical structure that gives it its name, "is begun from the two ends at once." Implicit in the poem he completed is the corollary recognition that a bridge has two ends, and that once the bridge is completed, what were its beginnings become its ends. The poem is thus not a summary of linear progress towards a goal, sought with difficulty but finally and firmly grasped. It is an attempt to diagram but regions of heaven, hell and purgatory within the poet's own mind; to find the right perspective from which to view those regions, and to find the proper discipline necessary to achieve that perspective. The quest takes us through time, from Columbus to Brooklyn, and through space, from "infinity's dim marge" to the depths of the tunnel; yet it never leaves the poet's own consciousness, which sounds at first like the music of the spheres, but on closer listening becomes "Whispers antiphonal in azure."

In a later poem, *The Broken Tower*, Crane expressed in two stanzas much of what I have been trying to say of *The Bridge*:

> *And so it was I entered the broken world*
> *To trace the visionary company of love, its voice*
> *An instant in the wind (I know not whither hurled)*
> *But not for long to hold each desperate choice.*

My word I poured. But was it cognate, scored
Of that tribunal monarch of the air
Whose thigh embronzes earth, strikes crystal Word
In wounds pledged once to hope—cleft to despair.

The Bridge is a record of the poet's attempt "to hold each desperate choice," and an outpouring of the poet's own word rather than the reception of an ultimate Word. Recognizing it as his own word, he can never know if it is cognate with that other Word. He can only build a broken tower up into the "visible wings of silence sown/ In azure circles" and *The Bridge,* failing its function as bridge, is that broken tower.

The criterion of success for a poem of this kind should not be whether or not the poet actually achieves the vision he seeks, or an absolute faith in the vision he has; nor should it be that the vision is acceptable to the reader. It should be the degree of poetic honesty and skill the poet exhibits in pursuing his quest. The quest itself may end in failure, or be a qualified success only. But regardless of that outcome the expression of a man as poet, trying by sheer will and desire, to find an acceptable purpose and meaning in his life, is still one of the most inspiring themes a poet can attempt. In an age which lacks any firm convictions, it may be the theme we must understand before we can understand ourselves.

1970   **THOMAS A. VOGLER**

AN INTRODUCTION BY WALDO FRANK

I dwell in Possibility
A fairer house than Prose,
More numerous of windows,
Superior of doors.
EMILY DICKINSON

a

AGRARIAN America had a common culture, which was both the fruit and the carrier of what I have called elsewhere "the great tradition."* This tradition rose in the Mediterranean world with the will of Egypt, Israel and Greece, to recreate the individual and the group in the image of values called divine. The same will established Catholic Europe, and when it failed (producing nonetheless what came to be the national European cultures), the great tradition survived. It survived in the Europe of Renaissance, Reformation, Revolution. With the Puritans, it was formally transplanted to the North American seaboard. Roger Williams, Thomas Hooker, Jonathan Edwards; later, in a more narrow sense, Jefferson, Madison, Adams, carried on the great tradition, with the same tools, on the same intellectual and economic terms, that had been brought from Europe and that had failed in Europe. It was transplanted, it was not transfigured. But before the final defeat of its Puritan avatar—a defeat ensured by the disappearance of our agra-

* *The Re-discovery of America.*

xvii

rian economy, the great tradition had borne fruit in two general forms. The first was the ideological art of what Lewis Mumford calls the Golden Day: a prophetic art of poets so diverse as Emerson, Thoreau, Poe, whose vision was one of Possibility and whose doom, since its premise was a disappearing world, was to remain suspended in the thin air of aspiration. The second was within the lives of the common people. Acceptance of the ideal of the great tradition had its effect upon their character; and this humbler achievement is recorded, perhaps finally, in the poems of Robert Frost. Frost's art, unlike Whitman's or Melville's, is one of Probability. It gives us not a vision, but *persons*. They are frustrated, poor, often mad. They face grimly their resurgent hills, knowing the failure of their lives to enact the beauty of their great tradition. Yet their dwelling within it for many generations, their acceptance of its will for their own, has given them even in defeat a fibre of strength, a smoldering spark of victory; and it is this in the verse of Frost that makes it poetry of a high order.

Frost's record (*North of Boston,* 1914; *Mountain Interval,* 1916) was already made when the United States entered the War; and the War brought final ruin to the American culture of "free" individuals living for the most part on farms, whose beauty Frost recorded. The tradition which had tempered the persons in Frost's poems had already, before the Civil War, sung its last high Word in the old terms that were valid from Plato to Fichte. And this too was fitting, for the Civil War prepared the doom which the World War completed, of our agrarian class-culture. But the great tradition, unbroken from Hermes Trismegistus and

Moses, does not die. In a society transfigured by new scientific and economic forces, it too must be transfigured. The literature and philosophy of the past hundred years reveal many efforts at this transfiguration: in this common purpose, Marx and Nietzsche are brothers. The poetry of Whitman was still founded on the substances of the old order. The poetry of Hart Crane is a deliberate continuance of the great tradition in terms of our industrialized world.

If we bear in mind this purpose of Crane's work, we shall be better prepared to understand his methods, his content, his obscurity. We shall, of course, not seek the clear forms of a poet of Probability, like Frost. But we shall, also, not too widely trust Crane's kinship with the poets of the Emersonian era, whose tradition he immediately continues. They were all, like Crane, bards of Possibility rather than scribes of realisation. Yet they relied upon inherited forms . . . forms emotional, ethical, social, intellectual and religious, transplanted from Europe and not too deliquescent for their uses. Whitman's apocalypse rested on the politics of Jefferson and on the economics of the physiocrats of France. Emerson was content with the ideology of Plato and Buddha, his own class world not too radically differing from theirs. Even Emily Dickinson based her explosive doubts upon the permanent premise of a sheltered private garden, to which such as she could always meditatively retire. These conventional assumptions gave to these poets an accessible and communicable form; for we too have been nurtured on the words of that old order. But in Crane, none of the ideal landmarks, none of the formal securities, survive; therefore his language problem—the poet's need to find words at once to create and to communicate his vision—is acute. Crane, who began to write while Frost was perfecting his story, lived, instinctively at first, then with poignant awareness, in a world whose cant outlines of person, class, creed, value—still clear, however weak, in Emerson's Boston, Whitman's New York, Poe's Richmond—had dissolved. His vision was the timeless One of all the seers, and it binds him to the great tradition; but because of the time that fleshed him and that he needed, to substance his vision, he could not employ traditional concretions. He began, naked and brave, in a cultural chaos; and his attempt, with sound materials, to achieve poetic form, was ever close to chaos. What is clear in Crane, besides the intensity and the traditionalism of his creative will, is the impact of inchoate forces through which he rose to utterance. Cities, machines, the warring hungers of lonely and herded men, the passions released from defeated loyalties, were ever near to overwhelm the poet. To master them, he must form his Word unaided. In his lack of valid terms to express his relationship with life, Crane was a true culture-child; more completely than either Emily Dickinson or Blake, he was a child of modern man.

b

HAROLD HART CRANE was born in Garrettsville, Ohio, July 21, 1899. His parents, Clarence Arthur Crane and Grace Hart, were of the pioneer stock that trekked in covered wagons from New England to the Western Reserve. But his grandparents, on both sides, had already shifted from the farm to small town business; and Clarence A. Crane became a wealthy candy manufacturer in Cleveland. Here, the poet, an only child, lived from his tenth year. At thirteen, he was composing verse; at sixteen, in the words of Gorham Munson,* "he was writing on a level that Amy Lowell never rose from." In the winter of 1916, he went with his mother, who soon separated from her husband, to the Isle of Pines, south of Cuba, where his grandfather Hart had a fruit ranch; and this journey, which gave him his first experience of the sea, was cardinal in his growth. The following year, he was in New York; in contact with Margaret Anderson and Jane Heap, editors of *The Little Review;* tutoring for college; writing; already passionately and rather wildly living. At this time, two almost mutually exclusive tendencies divided the American literary scene. One was centered by Ezra Pound, Alfred Kreymborg, the imagists, Harriet Monroe's *Poetry* and *The Little Review;* the other was grouped about *The Seven Arts.* Young Crane was in vital touch with both. He was reading Marlowe, Donne, Rimbaud, Laforgue; but he was also finding inspiration in Whitman, Sherwood Anderson and Melville. His action, when the United States lurched into war, reveals the complexity of his interests. He decided not to go to college, and by his own choice, returned to Cleveland, to work as a common laborer in a munition plant and a shipyard on the Lake. He loved machines, the earth-tang of the workers. He was no poet in an ivory tower. But he also loved music; he wanted time to write, to meditate, to read. The conflict of desires led him, perhaps, to accept what seemed a comfortable compromise; a job in the candy business of his father where

---

* *Destinations,* 1928. The essay in this volume on Crane, written in 1925, is, so far as I know, the first important study of the poet.

he hoped to find some leisure without losing contact with the industrial world.

The elder Crane seems to have been a man of turbulent and twisted power, tough-fibred and wholly loyal to the gods of Commerce. He was sincerely outraged by the jest of fortune which had given him a poet for a son. Doubtless, he was bitter at his one child's siding with the mother in the family conflict; but under all, there was a secret emotional bond between the two, making for the ricochet of antagonism and attraction that lasted between them until the father's death, a year before the poet's. The candy magnate set to work to drive the "poetry nonsense" out of his boy. Hart became a candy salesman behind a counter, a soda-jerker, a shipping clerk. He received a minimum wage. Trusted employees were detailed to spy on him lest he read "poetry books" during work hours. Hart Crane escaped several times from the paternal yoke, usually to advertising jobs near home or in New York. And at last, in 1920, he decided to break with both Cleveland and his father.

His exquisite balance of nerves was already permanently impaired. The youthful poet, who had left a comfortable household to live with machines and rough men, who had shouldered "the curse of sundered parentage,"* who had tasted the strong drink of literature and war, carried within him a burden intricate and heavy, a burden hard to hold in equilibrium. Doubtless, the chaos of his personal life led him to rationalise that accessible tangent ease from the strain of balance, which excess use of alcohol invited. Yet there was a deeper cause for the dis-equilibrium which, when Crane was

* *The Bridge.*

thirty-two, was finally to break him from his love of life and destroy him.

Crane was a mystic. The mystic is a man who *knows,* by immediate experience, the organic continuity between his self and the cosmos. This experience, which is the normal fruit of sensitivity, becomes intense in a man whose native energy is great; and lest it turn into an overwhelming, shattering burden, it must be ruthlessly disciplined and ordered. The easiest defense from this mystic burden is of course the common one of denying the mystic experience altogether. An anti-mystical age like ours is simply one so innerly resourceless that it solves, by negation and aggressive repression, the problem of organic continuity between the self and a seemingly chaotic world—thus perpetuating the inward-and-outward chaos. The true solution is too arduous for most men: by self-knowledge and self-discipline, it is to achieve within one's self a stable nucleus to bear and finally transfigure the world's impinging chaos. For the nucleus within the self, as it is gradually revealed, is impersonal and cosmic; is indeed the dynamic key to order in the "outward" world. By this synthesis of his own burden, the mystic escapes from destruction and becomes a master. Crane did not personally achieve it. Yet he was too virile to deny the experience of continuity; he let the world pour in; and since his nuclear self was not disciplined to detachment from his nerves and passions, he lived exacerbated in a constant swing between ecstasy and exhaustion. Therefore, he needed the tangent release of excess drink and sexual indulgence.

The poet was clearer and shrewder than the man. His mind, grown strong, sought a poetic principle to integrate the exuberant flood of his impressions. The important poems,

anterior to *The Bridge,* and written between his nineteenth
and his twenty-fifth year, reveal this quest but not the finding.
As Allen Tate points out in his Introduction to *White Build-
ings* (1926), "a suitable theme" is lacking. The themes of
these poems are high enough. But, to quote Mr. Tate again:
"A series of Imagist poems is a series of worlds. The poems
of Hart Crane are facets of a single vision; they refer to a
central imagination, a single evaluating power, which is at
once the motive of the poetry and the form of its realisation."
This central imagination, wanting the unitary principle or
theme, wavers and breaks; turns back upon itself instead of
mastering the envisaged substance of the poem. That is why,
in this first group, a fragmentary part of a poem is sometimes
greater than the whole. And that is why it is at times im-
possible to transpose a series of images into the sense- and
thought-sequence that originally moved the poet and that
must be perceived in order to move the reader. The mediate
principle, coterminous with both the absolute image-logic of
the poem and the thought-logic of the poet, and illumining
the latter in the former, is imperfect. The first lines of his
White Buildings

> *As silent as a mirror is believed*
> *Realities plunge in silence by . . .*

are a superb expression of chaos, and of the poet's need to
integrate this chaos within the active mirror of self. Page after
page, "realities plunge by," only ephemerally framed in a
mirroring mood which alas! at once melts, itself, into the
turbulent procession. Objective reality exists in these poems
only as an oblique moving-inward to the poet's mood. But

xxiv

the mood is never, as in imagist or romantic verse, given for
and as itself. It is given only as a moving-outward toward
the objective world. Each lyric is a diapason between two
integers of a continuous one. But the integers (subjective and
objective) are almost never clear; the sole clarity is the bal-
ance of antithetical movements. This makes of the poem an
abstract, wavering, æsthetic body. There is not yet, as in the
later work, a conscious, substantiated theme or principle of
vision to stratify the interacting parts of the poem into an
immobile whole. But in the final six lyrics (*Voyages*) there
is the beginning of a synthesis attained by the symbolic use
of the Sea. The turbulent experiences of Crane's childhood
and youth are merged into a litany of the Sea.

> *You must not cross nor ever trust beyond it*
> *Spry cordage of your bodies to caresses*
> *Too lichen-faithful from too wide a breast.*
> *The bottom of the sea is cruel.*
>
> *—And yet this great wink of eternity,*
> *Of rimless floods, unfettered leewardings,*
> *Samite sheeted and processioned where*
> *Her undinal vast belly moonward bends,*
> *Laughing the rapt inflections of our love;*
>
> *Take this Sea, whose diapason knells*
> *On scrolls of silver snowy sentences,*
> *The sceptred terror of whose sessions rends*
> *As her demeanors motion well or ill,*
> *All but the pieties of lovers' hands.*

Here is the Sea, objective, huge, hostile, encompassing,
maternal.

> *—As if too brittle or too clear to touch!*
> *The cables of our sleep so swiftly filed,*
> *Already hang, shred ends from remembered stars.*
> *One frozen, trackless smile . . . What words*
> *Can strangle this deaf moonlight? For we*
> *Are overtaken. Now no cry, no sword*
> *Can fasten or deflect this tidal wedge,*
> *Slow tyranny of moonlight, moonlight loved*
> *And changed. . . .*

And

> *. . . Blue latitudes and levels of your eyes,—*

here, as William Carlos Williams has noted, is the Sea giving to the poet's love its rhythm and very substance.

Crane is using the symbol of the Sea as a principle of unity and release from the contradictions of personal existence; much as D. H. Lawrence used the symbol of perfect sexual union. Both, as poetic instruments for solving the mystic's burden, are romantic and unreal; both denote a return to a "beginning" before the life of reason, and a unity won by the refusal of human consciousness. Lawrence was satisfied with his symbol. Not Crane. His intellect was more robust, his art more rigorous. Crane knew the Sea—source of life, first Mother—as death to man; and that to woo it was death. *White Buildings* closes on the note of surrender. But the poet is ready to begin his quest again for a theme that shall integrate, not destroy, the multiple human world he loves.

In 1924, the poems of *White Buildings* written but unpublished, Crane was living at 110 Columbia Heights, Brooklyn, in range of the Harbor, the Bridge, the sea-sounds:

> *Gongs in white surplices, beshrouded wails,*
> *Far strum of fog horns. . . .*

And now the integrating theme came to him. By the fall of 1925, he had achieved the pattern of his Poem. He was working as a writer of advertising copy. He appealed successfully to Otto H. Kahn (his father, after he left Cleveland, gave him no financial assistance until the last years when his son's fame began to impress him); and with a generous purse he went to the Isle of Pines; then to Paris, Marseilles, writing and—at intervals—rather riotously living. The Poem was completed in December, 1929. In the interim, Crane had learned that the house where the vision of *The Bridge* first came to him and where he finished it, was once the property of Washington Roebling, and that the very room in which Crane lived had been employed by the paralysed engineer of Brooklyn Bridge as an observation tower to watch its construction. In the year when Crane first found his theme, Lewis Mumford was prophetically writing:

". . . beyond any other aspect of New York, I think, the Brooklyn Bridge has been a source of joy and inspiration to the artist. . . . All that the age had just cause for pride in—its advances in science, its skill in handling iron, its personal heroism in the face of dangerous industrial processes, its willingness to attempt the untried and the impossible—came to a head in the Brooklyn Bridge."*

The Bridge was published in April, 1930 (a limited first edition, inscribed to Otto H. Kahn, was issued earlier in Paris by the Black Sun Press). In 1931, Crane received a fellowship from the Guggenheim Foundation, and went to Mexico; his plan being to write a poem on the history of Montezuma, a variation on the American theme which *The Bridge* stated.

* *Sticks and Stones.*

The principle that Hart Crane had sought, to make him master of his sense of immediate continuity with a world overwhelmingly chaotic, gave him *The Bridge*. But in actual life, it did not sustain him. He had a literary method to apply the principle to his vision; he had no psychological method to apply it to his person. The symbol of the Sea—theme of retreat into the unity of immersion and of dissolution—still bespoke him, as it had finally bespoken the love experience in *White Buildings*. *The Bridge*, with its challenging synthesis of life, wherein all the modern multiverse is accepted and transfigured without loss into One, could not hold its poet. The poems later than *The Bridge*, despite their technical perfection, mark a retreat from the high position of that Poem back to the mood of *White Buildings*—a return from grappling with the elements of the industrial world back to the primal Mother world whose symbol is the tropic Sea.

It was not accidental that Crane's tender friendships were with boys who followed the Sea. And drink was the Sea's coadjutor; for it gave Crane release not, as with most men, from the burden of *separateness* from life, but from the more intolerable burden of *continuity* with life's chaos. The Sea had ebbed, while he stood high above it on his mythic Bridge; now again it was rising.

> *Here waves climb into dusk on gleaming mail;*
> *Invisible valves of the sea—locks, tendons*
> *Crested and creeping, troughing corridors...*

Nor was it accidental that Crane now chose to go to Mexico, where for a thousand years a cult of Death—personal immolation in a Nature ruthless and terrible as the Sea—has been practiced by a folk of genius.

While Crane sailed to Mexico, I was writing:

"Perhaps the earth of Mexico conspired to create the tragic mood of the Aztec, and to fulfill it in the Conquest from which modern Mexico was born. It is an earth unwieldy to man's pleasure. Titanic and volcanic mountains, mesetas of thin air, exuberant valleys, burning deserts, encourage a culture not smiling but extreme, from tears to frenzied laughter. This earth is a tyrant; it exiles valley from valley, it begrudges loam for corn or overwhelms it with torrential rains. Man is a stranger within it, and yet he loves it like a goddess, radiant, cruel, suddenly indulgent, in whose house he must serve forever. It is no mystery that in such an earth man should have built temples of blood or possessed his life in contemplation of a loveliness deadly as fire and distant as the stars.

"But this man was still man. In a hostile and adorable world, man's and woman's love of life breathed on. . . ."*

The second paragraph refers to the Mexico of Revolution —"the will of Mexico to be free of its death and of a beauty that flowers in death"; the first describes the Mexico that now possessed Hart Crane. The periodicity of his excesses grew swifter; the crystal intervening times when he could write were crowded out. Crane fought death in Mexico. But on his return to New York, to the modern chaos, there was the Sea: and he could not resist it.

On April 27, 1932, a few moments before noon, he walked to the stern of the *Orizaba*. The boat was about three hundred miles north of Havana, leaving the warm waters which fifteen years before he had first known. He took off his coat, quietly, and leaped.

c

THE beauty of most of Crane's lyrics and of many passages in *The Bridge* seems to me to be inviolable. If I begin to analyse

* *America Hispana.*

this conviction, I am brought first to the poetic texture. Its traditional base is complex. Here is a music plainly related to the Elizabethans. And here, also, is a sturdy lilt, like the march of those equal children of the Elizabethans—the pioneers. Although Crane describes a modern cabaret,

> *Brazen hypnotics glitter here;*
> *Glee shifts from foot to foot . . .*

always, there is this homely metronomic, linking him to his fathers. Hence the organic soundness of the verse. Its living-ness it owes to the dimension of variant emergence from the traditional music—like the emergence of our industrial world from the base of old America. Indeed, the entire intellectual and spiritual content of Crane's verse, and of Crane the child of modern man, could be derived from a study of his typical texture. And this is earnest of his importance.

But an analysis of Crane's poetics does not belong in a brief introduction. More fitting, perhaps, will be a swift out-line of the action of *The Bridge,* if it help the reader to give his whole attention at once to that Poem's inner substance.

The will of Crane in *The Bridge* becomes deliberately myth-making. But this will, as we have seen, is born of a desperate, personal need: the poet *must* create order from the chaos with which his associative genius overwhelms him. The Poem retains the personal origin of its own will. The revelation of *The Bridge,* as myth and principle, comes to a person in the course of his day's business; and that person is the poet. In this sense, *The Bridge* is allied to the *Commedia* of Dante who also, in response to desperate need, takes a journey in the course of which his need finds consummation.

NOTION OF JOURNEY

Lest the analogy be misleading, I immediately amend it. Dante's cosmos, imaged in an age of cultural maturity, when the life of man was coterminous with his vision, contains Time and persons: only in the ecstatic last scenes of the *Paradiso* are they momently merged and lost. Therefore, the line of Dante's Poem is always clear, being forth and back in Time: and the focus of the action is always cogent, being the person of the Poet with whom the reader can readily graph points of reference. Crane's cosmos (for reasons which we examined when we called Crane a child of modern man, a poet innocent of culture-words) has no Time: and his person-sense is vacillant and evanescent. Crane's journey is that of an individual unsure of his own form and lost to Time. This difference at once clarifies the disadvantageous æsthetic of *The Bridge,* as compared with that of broadly analogous Poems of cosmic search, like the *Commedia* or *Don Quixote.* It exemplifies the rôle played by the cultural epoch in the creation of even the most personal work of genius.

In *Proem,* the poet exhorts the object of his choice—the Bridge. It shall synthesise the world of chaos. It joins city, river, and sea; man made it with his new Hand, the machine. And parabolawise, it shall now vault the continent and, transmuted, reach that inward heaven which is the fulfillment of man's need of order. Part One, *Ave Maria,* is the vision of Columbus, mystic navigator who mapped his voyage in Isaiah, seeking to weld the world's riven halves into one. But this Columbus is scarcely a person; he is suffused in his history and his ocean; his will is more substantial than his eye. Nor does he live in Time. Part Two, *Powhatan's Daughter* (the Indian Princess is the flesh of America, the American earth, and mother of our dream), begins the recital of the poet's journey which in turn traces in extension (as Columbus in essence) the myth's trajectory. The poet awakes in his room above the Harbor, beside his lover. Risen (taking the harbor and the sea-sounds with him), he walks through the lowly Brooklyn streets: but walks with his cultural past: Pizzaro, Cortés, Priscilla, and now Rip Van Winkle whose eyes, fresh from sleep, will abide the poet's as they approach the transfigured world of today. He descends the subway that tunnels the East River (the Bridge is above); and now the subway is a river "leaping" from Far Rockaway to Golden Gate. A river of steel rails at first, bearing westward America's urban civilisation ("Stick your patent name on a signboard") and waking as it runs the burdened trudge of pioneers and all their worlds of factory and song. The patterning march of the American settlers traces the body, gradually, of Pocahontas; the flow of continent and man becomes the Great River; the huge travail of continental life, after the white man and before him, is borne southward, "meeting the Gulf." Powhatan's daughter, America's flesh, dances and the flesh becomes spirit. Dances the poet's boyhood memories of star and lake, of "sleek boat nibbling margin grass"; dances at last into the life of an Indiana mother, home from a frustrate trek to California for gold, who is bidding her son farewell; he is going east again to follow the sea. ("Write me from Rio.")

There are no persons in the universe, barely emergent from chaos, of Hart Crane; and this first crystallisation—the prairie mother—is the first weak block in the Poem's structure. Now with Part Three, *Cutty Sark,* the physical course of the poet (the subway ride has exploded into the cosmic implications of the River) returns to view, but blurred. The poet is in South Street, Manhattan, near midnight: he is carousing with a sailor who brings him, in snatches of song, Leviathan, Plato, Stamboul—and the dim harbinger of Atlantis. "I started walking home across the Bridge"; and there, in the hallucinatory parade of clippers who once winked round the Horn "bright skysails ticketing the Line," the poet is out again, now seaward.

Part Four, *Cape Hatteras,* is the turning point of the Poem. Thus far, we have seen the individual forms of the poet's crowded day melt into widening, deepening cycles of association. Columbus into the destiny and will of the Atlantic: two lovers into the harbor, the harbor into the sea: a subway into a transcontinental railroad, into a continent, into a River; the River into the Gulf; the Indian princess into the Earth Mother and her dance into the tumult and traffic of the nation; ribald South Street into a vision—while the Bridge brings the clippers that bring China—of Atlantis. Now, the movement turns back toward crystallisation. *Cape Hatteras* at first invokes the geologic age that lifted the Appalachians above the waters; the cosmic struggle sharpens into the birth of the airplane—industrial America; the "red, eternal flesh of Pocahontas" gives us, finally, Walt Whitman. "Years of the Modern! Propulsions toward what capes?" The Saunterer on the Open Road takes the hand of the poet. Part Five, *Three Songs,* is a pause for humbler music, upon the variable theme of woman. Part Six, *Quaker Hill,* is an attempt to focus the cosmic journey once more upon the person of the poet. In my judgment, it fails for the same basic reasons. And now, Part Seven, *The Tunnel,* runs swift and fatefully to the climax. The poet, in mid air at midnight, leaves the Bridge; he "comes down to earth" and returns home as he had left, by subway.

This unreal collapse of bridge into subway has meaning. The subway is the tunnel; is the whole life of the city entextured of all the images created by the Poem, all the previous apparitions of earth and sun. The tunnel is America, and is a kind of hell. But it has dynamic direction, it is moving! In the plunging subway darkness, appears Poe:

> *And why do I often meet your visage here,*
> *Your eyes like agate lanterns . . . ?*

If the reader understands Poe, he will understand the apparition. Of all the classic poets of the great tradition in America, Poe—perhaps the least as artist—was the most advanced, the most prophetic as thinker. All, as we have noted, were content more or less with the merely transplanted terms of an agrarian culture. Only Poe guessed the transfiguring effect of the Machine upon the forms of human life, upon the very concept of the person. The Tunnel gives us man in his industrial hell which the machine—his hand and heart—has made; now let the machine be his godlike Hand to uplift him! The plunging subway shall merge with the vaulting bridge. Whitman gives the vision; Poe, however vaguely, the method. The final part, *Atlantis,* is a transposed return to the beginning. The Bridge, in Time, has linked Atlantis with Cathay. Now it becomes an absolute experience. Like any human event, *fully known,* it links man instantaneously, "beyond time," with the Truth.

d

THE structural pattern of *The Bridge* is superb: a man moves of a morning from Brooklyn to Manhattan, returns at midnight, each stage of his course adumbrating, by the mystic law of continuity, into American figures with cosmic overtones; and all caught up in a mythic bridge whose functional span is a parabola and an immediate act of vision. The flaw lies in the weakness of the personal crystallisation upon which the vision rests, as the Bridge is spanned upon its piers. This flaw gets into the idiom and texture. Sometimes the image blurs, the sequence breaks, the plethora of words is blinding. There is even, in the development of certain figures, a tendency toward inflation which one is tempted to connect with the febrile, false ebullience of the American epoch (1924-1929) in which the Poem was written. Yet the concept is sound; the poet's genius has on the whole equalled his ambition. Even the failings in execution, since they are due to weakness of the personal focus, help to express the epoch; for it is in the understanding and creating of *persons* that our rapidly collectivising age is poorest.

Crane's myth must, of course, not be confused with the myth as we find it in Homer or the Bible or the Nibelungen. The Bridge is not a particularised being to be popularly sung; it is a conceptual symbol to be *used*. And the fact that this symbol begins as a man-constructed thing is of the essence of its truth for our instrumental age. From a machine-made entity, the Poem makes the Bridge into a machine. But it has beauty. This means that through the men who builded it, the life of America has flowed into the Bridge—the life of our past *and our future*. A cosmic content has given beauty to the Bridge; now it must give it a poetic function. From being a machine of body, it becomes an instrument of spirit. *The Bridge is matter made into human action.*

We may confidently say that this message of *The Bridge* will be more comprehensible in the future (not in the immediate future), when the functionally limited materialism of our collectivist era has, through success, grown inadequate to the deepened needs of a mankind released from economic insecurity and prepared, by leisure, for regeneration. For even as necessity, today and tomorrow, drives most men to think collectively in order that they may survive; necessity, day after tomorrow, will drive men to think personally (poetically, cosmically), in order that their survival may have meaning. When the collectivist era has done its work—the abolition of economic classes and of animal want—men will turn, as only the privileged of the past could ever turn, toward the discovery of Man.

But when that time comes, the message of *The Bridge* will be taken for granted; it will be too obvious, even as today it is too obscure, for general interest. The revelation in Crane's poems, however, of a man who through the immediate conduit of his senses experienced the organic unity between his self, the objective world, and the cosmos, will be accepted as a great human value. And the poems, whose very texture reveals and sings this man, will be remembered.

1932

TO
✦BROOKLYN BRIDGE

How many dawns, chill from his rippling rest
The seagull's wings shall dip and pivot him,
Shedding white rings of tumult, building high
Over the chained bay waters Liberty —

Then, with inviolate curve, forsake our eyes
As apparitional as sails that cross
Some page of figures to be filed away;
— Till elevators drop us from our day . . .

I think of cinemas, panoramic sleights
With multitudes bent toward some flashing scene
Never disclosed, but hastened to again,
Foretold to other eyes on the same screen;

And Thee, across the harbor, silver-paced
As though the sun took step of thee, yet left
Some motion ever unspent in thy stride,—
Implicitly thy freedom staying thee!

Out of some subway scuttle, cell or loft
A bedlamite speeds to thy parapets,
Tilting there momently, shrill shirt ballooning,
A jest falls from the speechless caravan.

Down Wall, from girder into street noon leaks,
A rip-tooth of the sky's acetylene;
All afternoon the cloud-flown derricks turn . . .
Thy cables breathe the North Atlantic still.

And obscure as that heaven of the Jews,
Thy guerdon . . . Accolade thou dost bestow
Of anonymity time cannot raise:
Vibrant reprieve and pardon thou dost show.

O harp and altar, of the fury fused,
(How could mere toil align thy choiring strings!)
Terrific threshold of the prophet's pledge,
Prayer of pariah, and the lover's cry,—

Again the traffic lights that skim thy swift
Unfractioned idiom, immaculate sigh of stars,
Beading thy path — condense eternity:
And we have seen night lifted in thine arms.

Under thy shadow by the piers I waited;
Only in darkness is thy shadow clear.
The City's fiery parcels all undone,
Already snow submerges an iron year . . .

O Sleepless as the river under thee,
Vaulting the sea, the prairies' dreaming sod,
Unto us lowliest sometime sweep, descend
And of the curveship lend a myth to God.

I

AVE MARIA

Venient annis, sæcula seris,
Quibus Oceanus vincula rerum
Laxet et ingens pateat tellus
Tiphysque novos detegat orbes
Nec sit terris ultima Thule.
—SENECA

⚔ AVE MARIA

BE with me, Luis de San Angel, now —
Witness before the tides can wrest away
The word I bring, O you who reined my suit
Into the Queen's great heart that doubtful day;
For I have seen now what no perjured breath
Of clown nor sage can riddle or gainsay; —
To you, too, Juan Perez, whose counsel fear
And greed adjourned,— I bring you back Cathay!

*Columbus,
alone, gazing
toward Spain,
invokes the
presence of
two faithful
partisans of
his quest . . .*

Here waves climb into dusk on gleaming mail;
Invisible valves of the sea,— locks, tendons
Crested and creeping, troughing corridors
That fall back yawning to another plunge.
Slowly the sun's red caravel drops light
Once more behind us. . . . It is morning there —
O where our Indian emperies lie revealed,
Yet lost, all, let this keel one instant yield!

I thought of Genoa; and this truth, now proved,
That made me exile in her streets, stood me

5

More absolute than ever — biding the moon
Till dawn should clear that dim frontier, first seen
— The Chan's great continent. . . . Then faith, not **fear**
Nigh surged me witless. . . . Hearing the surf near —
I, wonder-breathing, kept the watch,— saw
The first palm chevron the first lighted hill.

And lowered. And they came out to us crying,
"The Great White Birds!" (O Madre María, still
One ship of these thou grantest safe returning;
Assure us through thy mantle's ageless blue!)
And record of more, floating in a casque,
Was tumbled from us under bare poles scudding;
And later hurricanes may claim more pawn. . . .
For here between two worlds, another, harsh,

This third, of water, tests the word; lo, here
Bewilderment and mutiny heap whelming
Laughter, and shadow cuts sleep from the **heart**
Almost as though the Moor's flung scimitar
Found more than flesh to fathom in its fall.
Yet under tempest-lash and surfeitings
Some inmost sob, half-heard, dissuades the abyss,
Merges the wind in measure to the waves,

Series on series, infinite,— till eyes" 2
Starved wide on blackened tides, accrete — enclose
This turning rondure whole, this crescent ring
Sun-cusped and zoned with modulated fire
Like pearls that whisper through the Doge's hands
— Yet no delirium of jewels! O Fernando,

Take of that eastern shore, this western sea,
Yet yield thy God's, thy Virgin's charity!

— Rush down the plenitude, and you shall see
Isaiah counting famine on this lee!

.   .   .

An herb, a stray branch among salty teeth,
The jellied weeds that drag the shore,— perhaps
Tomorrow's moon will grant us Saltes Bar —
Palos again,— a land cleared of long war.
Some Angelus environs the cordage tree;
Dark waters onward shake the dark prow free.

.   .   .

O Thou who sleepest on Thyself, apart
Like ocean athwart lanes of death and birth,
And all the eddying breath between dost search
Cruelly with love thy parable of man,—
Inquisitor! incognizable Word
Of Eden and the enchained Sepulchre,
Into thy steep savannahs, burning blue,
Utter to loneliness the sail is true.

Who grindest oar, and arguing the mast
Subscribest holocaust of ships, O Thou
Within whose primal scan consummately
The glistening seignories of Ganges swim; —
Who sendest greeting by the corposant,

And Teneriffe's garnet — flamed it in a cloud,
Urging through night our passage to the Chan;—
Te Deum laudamus, for thy teeming span!

Of all that amplitude that time explores,
A needle in the sight, suspended north,—
Yielding by inference and discard, faith
And true appointment from the hidden shoal:
This disposition that thy night relates
From Moon to Saturn in one sapphire wheel:
The orbic wake of thy once whirling feet,
Elohim, still I hear thy sounding heel!

White toil of heaven's cordons, mustering
In holy rings all sails charged to the far
Hushed gleaming fields and pendant seething wheat
Of knowledge,— round thy brows unhooded now
— The kindled Crown! acceded of the poles
And biassed by full sails, meridians reel
Thy purpose — still one shore beyond desire!
The sea's green crying towers a-sway, Beyond

And kingdoms
                   naked in the
                              trembling heart —
     Te Deum laudamus
                         O Thou Hand of Fire

II

POWHATAN'S DAUGHTER

" — *Pocahuntus, a well-featured but wanton yong girle . . . of the age of eleven or twelve years, get the boyes forth with her into the market place, and make them wheele, falling on their hands, turning their heels upwards, whom she would followe, and wheele so herself, naked as she was, all the fort over.*"

⭐THE HARBOR DAWN

INSISTENTLY through sleep — a tide of voices —
They meet you listening midway in your dream,
The long, tired sounds, fog-insulated noises:
Gongs in white surplices, beshrouded wails,
Far strum of fog horns . . . signals dispersed in veils.

*400 years and
more . . . or is
it from the
soundless shore
of sleep that
time*

And then a truck will lumber past the wharves
As winch engines begin throbbing on some deck;
Or a drunken stevedore's howl and thud below
Comes echoing alley-upward through dim snow.

And if they take your sleep away sometimes
They give it back again. Soft sleeves of sound
Attend the darkling harbor, the pillowed bay;
Somewhere out there in blankness steam

Spills into steam, and wanders, washed away
— Flurried by keen fifings, eddied
Among distant chiming buoys — adrift. The sky,

Cool feathery fold, suspends, distills
This wavering slumber. . . . Slowly —
Immemorially the window, the half-covered chair
Ask nothing but this sheath of pallid air.

recalls you to your love, there in a waking dream to merge your seed

And you beside me, blessèd now while sirens
Sing to us, stealthily weave us into day —
Serenely now, before day claims our eyes
Your cool arms murmurously about me lay.

While myriad snowy hands are clustering at the
panes —

> *your hands within my hands are deeds;*
> *my tongue upon your throat — singing*
> *arms close; eyes wide, undoubtful*
> *dark*
> *drink the dawn —*
> *a forest shudders in your hair!*

— with whom?

The window goes blond slowly. Frostily clears.
From Cyclopean towers across Manhattan waters
— Two — three bright window-eyes aglitter, disk
The sun, released — aloft with cold gulls hither.

Who is the woman with us in the dawn? . . . whose is the flesh our feet have moved upon?

The fog leans one last moment on the sill.
Under the mistletoe of dreams, a star —
As though to join us at some distant hill —
Turns in the waking west and goes to sleep.

12

VAN WINKLE

Macadam, gun-grey as the tunny's belt,
Leaps from Far Rockaway to Golden Gate:
Listen! the miles a hurdy-gurdy grinds —
Down gold arpeggios mile on mile unwinds.

*Streets spread
past store and
factory — sped
by sunlight
and her
smile . . .*

Times earlier, when you hurried off to school,
— It is the same hour though a later day —
You walked with Pizarro in a copybook,
And Cortes rode up, reining tautly in —
Firmly as coffee grips the taste,— and away!

There was Priscilla's cheek close in the wind,
And Captain Smith, all beard and certainty,
And Rip Van Winkle bowing by the way,—
"Is this Sleepy Hollow, friend — ?" And he —

*Like Memory,
she is time's
truant, shall
take you by
the hand . . .*

*And Rip forgot the office hours,
          and he forgot the pay;
Van Winkle sweeps a tenement
          way down on Avenue A,—*

13

The grind-organ says . . . Remember, remember
The cinder pile at the end of the backyard
Where we stoned the family of young
Garter snakes under . . . And the monoplanes
We launched — with paper wings and twisted
Rubber bands . . . Recall — recall

                                    the rapid tongues
That flittered from under the ash heap day
After day whenever your stick discovered
Some sunning inch of unsuspecting fibre —
It flashed back at your thrust, as clean as fire.

And Rip was slowly made aware
       that he, Van Winkle, was not here
           nor there. He woke and swore he'd seen Broadway
               a Catskill daisy chain in May —

So memory, that strikes a rhyme out of a box,
Or splits a random smell of flowers through glass —
Is it the whip stripped from the lilac tree
One day in spring my father took to me,
Or is it the Sabbatical, unconscious smile
My mother almost brought me once from church
And once only, as I recall — ?

It flickered through the snow screen, blindly
It forsook her at the doorway, it was gone
Before I had left the window. It
Did not return with the kiss in the hall.

Macadam, gun-grey as the tunny's belt,
Leaps from Far Rockaway to Golden Gate. . . .
Keep hold of that nickel for car-change, Rip,—
Have you got your *"Times"* —?
And hurry along, Van Winkle — it's getting late!

⚔ THE RIVER

*... and past
the din and
slogans of
the year —*

Stick your patent name on a signboard
brother — all over — going west — young man
Tintex — Japalac — Certain-teed Overalls ads
and lands sakes! under the new playbill ripped
in the guaranteed corner — see Bert Williams what?
Minstrels when you steal a chicken just
save me the wing for if it isn't
Erie it ain't for miles around a
Mazda — and the telegraphic night coming on Thomas

a Ediford — and whistling down the tracks
a headlight rushing with the sound — can you
imagine — while an EXPRESS makes time like
SCIENCE — COMMERCE and the HOLYGHOST
RADIO ROARS IN EVERY HOME WE HAVE THE NORTHPOLE
WALLSTREET AND VIRGINBIRTH WITHOUT STONES OR
WIRES OR EVEN RUNNING brooks connecting ears
and no more sermons windows flashing roar
breathtaking — as you like it ... eh?

So the 20th Century — so
whizzed the Limited — roared by and left
three men, still hungry on the tracks, ploddingly
watching the tail lights wizen and converge, slip-
ping gimleted and neatly out of sight.

.   .   .   .   .   .

The last bear, shot drinking in the Dakotas
Loped under wires that span the mountain stream.
Keen instruments, strung to a vast precision
Bind town to town and dream to ticking dream.   *to those*
But some men take their liquor slow — and count   *whose addresses*
— Though they'll confess no rosary nor clue —   *are never near*
The river's minute by the far brook's year.
Under a world of whistles, wires and steam
Caboose-like they go ruminating through
Ohio, Indiana — blind baggage —
To Cheyenne tagging . . . Maybe Kalamazoo.

Time's rendings, time's blendings they construe
As final reckonings of fire and snow;
Strange bird-wit, like the elemental gist
Of unwalled winds they offer, singing low
My Old Kentucky Home and *Casey Jones,*
Some Sunny Day. I heard a road-gang chanting so.
And afterwards, who had a colt's eyes — one said,
"Jesus! Oh I remember watermelon days!" And sped
High in a cloud of merriment, recalled
" — And when my Aunt Sally Simpson smiled," he drawled —
"It was almost Louisiana, long ago."

17

"There's no place like Booneville though, Buddy,"
One said, excising a last burr from his vest,
" — For early trouting." Then peering in the can,
" — But I kept on the tracks." Possessed, resigned,
He trod the fire down pensively and grinned,
Spreading dry shingles of a beard. . . .

                                    Behind

My father's cannery works I used to see
Rail-squatters ranged in nomad raillery,
The ancient men — wifeless or runaway
Hobo-trekkers that forever search
An empire wilderness of freight and rails.
Each seemed a child, like me, on a loose perch,
Holding to childhood like some termless play.
John, Jake or Charley, hopping the slow freight
 — Memphis to Tallahassee — riding the rods,
Blind fists of nothing, humpty-dumpty clods.

Yet they touch something like a key perhaps.
From pole to pole across the hills, the states
but who have   — They know a body under the wide rain;
touched her,
knowing her   Youngsters with eyes like fjords, old reprobates
without name   With racetrack jargon,— dotting immensity
They lurk across her, knowing her yonder breast
Snow-silvered, sumac-stained or smoky blue —
Is past the valley-sleepers, south or west.
 — As I have trod the rumorous midnights, too,

And past the circuit of the lamp's thin flame
(O Nights that brought me to her body bare!)

Have dreamed beyond the print that bound her name.
Trains sounding the long blizzards out — I heard
Wail into distances I knew were hers.
Papooses crying on the wind's long mane
Screamed redskin dynasties that fled the brain,
— Dead echoes! But I knew her body there,
Time like a serpent down her shoulder, dark,
And space, an eaglet's wing, laid on her hair.

Under the Ozarks, domed by Iron Mountain,
The old gods of the rain lie wrapped in pools
Where eyeless fish curvet a sunken fountain
And re-descend with corn from querulous crows.
Such pilferings make up their timeless eatage,
Propitiate them for their timber torn
By iron, iron — always the iron dealt cleavage!
They doze now, below axe and powder horn.

*nor the
myths of her
fathers . . .*

And Pullman breakfasters glide glistening steel
From tunnel into field — iron strides the dew —
Straddles the hill, a dance of wheel on wheel.
You have a half-hour's wait at Siskiyou,
Or stay the night and take the next train through.
Southward, near Cairo passing, you can see
The Ohio merging,— borne down Tennessee;
And if it's summer and the sun's in dusk
Maybe the breeze will lift the River's musk
— As though the waters breathed that you might know
Memphis Johnny, Steamboat Bill, Missouri Joe.
Oh, lean from the window, if the train slows down,
As though you touched hands with some ancient clown,

— A little while gaze absently below
And hum *Deep River* with them while they go.

Yes, turn again and sniff once more — look see,
O Sheriff, Brakeman and Authority —
Hitch up your pants and crunch another quid,
For you, too, feed the River timelessly.
And few evade full measure of their fate;
Always they smile out eerily what they seem.
I could believe he joked at heaven's gate —
Dan Midland — jolted from the cold brake-beam.

Down, down — born pioneers in time's despite,
Grimed tributaries to an ancient flow —
They win no frontier by their wayward plight,
But drift in stillness, as from Jordan's brow.

You will not hear it as the sea; even stone
Is not more hushed by gravity . . . But slow,
As loth to take more tribute — sliding prone
Like one whose eyes were buried long ago

The River, spreading, flows — and spends your dream.
What are you, lost within this tideless spell?
You are your father's father, and the stream —
A liquid theme that floating niggers swell.

Damp tonnage and alluvial march of days —
Nights turbid, vascular with silted shale
And roots surrendered down of moraine clays:
The Mississippi drinks the farthest dale.

O quarrying passion, undertowed sunlight!
The basalt surface drags a jungle grace
Ochreous and lynx-barred in lengthening might;
Patience! and you shall reach the biding place!

Over De Soto's bones the freighted floors
Throb past the City storied of three thrones.
Down two more turns the Mississippi pours
(Anon tall ironsides up from salt lagoons)

And flows within itself, heaps itself free.
All fades but one thin skyline 'round . . . Ahead
No embrace opens but the stinging sea;
The River lifts itself from its long bed,

Poised wholly on its dream, a mustard glow
Tortured with history, its one will — flow!
— The Passion spreads in wide tongues, choked and slow,
Meeting the Gulf, hosannas silently below.

THE DANCE

*Then you shall
see her truly
— your blood
remembering
its first
invasion of her
secrecy, its
first encounters
with her kin,
her chieftain
lover . . . his
shade that
haunts the
lakes and hills*

The swift red flesh, a winter king —
Who squired the glacier woman down the sky?
She ran the neighing canyons all the spring;
She spouted arms; she rose with maize — to die.

And in the autumn drouth, whose burnished hands
With mineral wariness found out the stone
Where prayers, forgotten, streamed the mesa sands?
He holds the twilight's dim, perpetual throne.

Mythical brows we saw retiring — loth,
Disturbed and destined, into denser green.
Greeting they sped us, on the arrow's oath:
Now lie incorrigibly what years between. . .

There was a bed of leaves, and broken play;
There was a veil upon you, Pocahontas, bride —
O Princess whose brown lap was virgin May;
And bridal flanks and eyes hid tawny pride.

I left the village for dogwood. By the canoe
Tugging below the mill-race, I could see
Your hair's keen crescent running, and the blue
First moth of evening take wing stealthily.

What laughing chains the water wove and threw!
I learned to catch the trout's moon whisper; I
Drifted how many hours I never knew,
But, watching, saw that fleet young crescent die,—

And one star, swinging, take its place, alone,
Cupped in the larches of the mountain pass —
Until, immortally, it bled into the dawn.
I left my sleek boat nibbling margin grass...

I took the portage climb, then chose
A further valley-shed; I could not stop.
Feet nozzled wat'ry webs of upper flows;
One white veil gusted from the very top.

O Appalachian Spring! I gained the ledge;
Steep, inaccessible smile that eastward bends
And northward reaches in that violet wedge
Of Adirondacks! — wisped of azure wands,

Over how many bluffs, tarns, streams I sped!
— And knew myself within some boding shade: —
Grey tepees tufting the blue knolls ahead,
Smoke swirling through the yellow chestnut glade...

A distant cloud, a thunder-bud — it grew,
That blanket of the skies: the padded foot
Within,— I heard it; 'til its rhythm drew,
— Siphoned the black pool from the heart's hot root!

A cyclone threshes in the turbine crest,
Swooping in eagle feathers down your back;
Know, Maquokeeta, greeting; know death's best;
— Fall, Sachem, strictly as the tamarack!

A birch kneels. All her whistling fingers fly.
The oak grove circles in a crash of leaves;
The long moan of a dance is in the sky.
Dance, Maquokeeta: Pocahontas grieves . . .

And every tendon scurries toward the twangs
Of lightning deltaed down your saber hair.
Now snaps the flint in every tooth; red fangs
And splay tongues thinly busy the blue air . . .

Dance, Maquokeeta! snake that lives before,
That casts his pelt, and lives beyond! Sprout, horn!
Spark, tooth! Medicine-man, relent, restore —
Lie to us,— dance us back the tribal morn!

Spears and assemblies: black drums thrusting on —
O yelling battlements,— I, too, was liege
To rainbows currying each pulsant bone:
Surpassed the circumstance, danced out the siege!

And buzzard-circleted, screamed from the stake;
I could not pick the arrows from my side.
Wrapped in that fire, I saw more escorts wake —
Flickering, sprint up the hill groins like a tide.

I heard the hush of lava wrestling your arms,
And stag teeth foam about the raven throat;

Flame cataracts of heaven in seething swarms
Fed down your anklets to the sunset's moat.

O, like the lizard in the furious noon,
That drops his legs and colors in the sun,
— And laughs, pure serpent, Time itself, and moon
Of his own fate, I saw thy change begun!

And saw thee dive to kiss that destiny
Like one white meteor, sacrosanct and blent
At last with all that's consummate and free
There, where the first and last gods keep thy tent.

.   .   .   .

Thewed of the levin, thunder-shod and lean,
Lo, through what infinite seasons dost thou gaze —
Across what bivouacs of thine angered slain,
And see'st thy bride immortal in the maize!

Totem and fire-gall, slumbering pyramid —
Though other calendars now stack the sky,
Thy freedom is her largesse, Prince, and hid
On paths thou knewest best to claim her by.

High unto Labrador the sun strikes free
Her speechless dream of snow, and stirred again,
She is the torrent and the singing tree;
And she is virgin to the last of men . . .

West, west and south! winds over Cumberland
And winds across the llano grass resume
Her hair's warm sibilance. Her breasts are fanned
O stream by slope and vineyard — into bloom!

And when the caribou slant down for salt
Do arrows thirst and leap? Do antlers shine
Alert, star-triggered in the listening vault
Of dusk? — And are her perfect brows to thine?

We danced, O Brave, we danced beyond their farms,
In cobalt desert closures made our vows . . .
Now is the strong prayer folded in thine arms,
The serpent with the eagle in the boughs.

INDIANA

The morning glory, climbing the morning long
   Over the lintel on its wiry vine,
Closes before the dusk, furls in its song
      As I close mine. . .

*. . . and read
her in a
mother's
farewell gaze.*

And bison thunder rends my dreams no more
   As once my womb was torn, my boy, when you
Yielded your first cry at the prairie's door. . .
      Your father knew

Then, though we'd buried him behind us, far
   Back on the gold trail — then his lost bones stirred. . .
But you who drop the scythe to grasp the oar
      Knew not, nor heard

How we, too, Prodigal, once rode off, too —
   Waved Seminary Hill a gay good-bye. . .
We found God lavish there in Colorado
      But passing sly.

The pebbles sang, the firecat slunk away
   And glistening through the sluggard freshets came

In golden syllables loosed from the clay
     His gleaming name.

A dream called Eldorado was his town,
    It rose up shambling in the nuggets' wake,
It had no charter but a promised crown
     Of claims to stake.

But we,— too late, too early, howsoever —
    Won nothing out of fifty-nine — those years —
But gilded promise, yielded to us never,
     And barren tears. . .

The long trail back! I huddled in the shade
    Of wagon-tenting looked out once and saw
Bent westward, passing on a stumbling jade
     A homeless squaw —

Perhaps a halfbreed. On her slender back
    She cradled a babe's body, riding without rein.
Her eyes, strange for an Indian's, were not black
     But sharp with pain

And like twin stars. They seemed to shun the gaze
    Of all our silent men — the long team line —
Until she saw me — when their violet haze
     Lit with love shine. . .

I held you up — I suddenly the bolder,
    Knew that mere words could not have brought us nearer.
She nodded — and that smile across her shoulder
     Will still endear her

As long as Jim, your father's memory, is warm.
   Yes, Larry, now you're going to sea, remember
You were the first — before Ned and this farm,—
      First-born, remember —

And since then — all that's left to me of Jim
   Whose folks, like mine, came out of Arrowhead.
And you're the only one with eyes like him —
      Kentucky bred!

I'm standing still, I'm old, I'm half of stone!
   Oh, hold me in those eyes' engaging blue;
There's where the stubborn years gleam and atone,—
      Where gold is true!

Down the dim turnpike to the river's edge —
   Perhaps I'll hear the mare's hoofs to the ford. . .
Write me from Rio . . . and you'll keep your pledge;
      I know your word!

Come back to Indiana — not too late!
   (Or will you be a ranger to the end?)
Good-bye. . . Good-bye. . . oh, I shall always wait
   You, Larry, traveller —
                    stranger,
                          son,
                                — my friend —

III

CUTTY SARK

O, the navies old and oaken,
O, the Temeraire no more!
— MELVILLE

λ CUTTY SARK

I MET a man in South Street, tall —
a nervous shark tooth swung on his chain.
His eyes pressed through green glass
— green glasses, or bar lights made them
so —
      shine —
                GREEN —
                        eyes —
stepped out — forgot to look at you
or left you several blocks away —

in the nickel-in-the-slot piano jogged
"Stamboul Nights" — weaving somebody's nickel — sang —

    O Stamboul Rose — dreams weave the rose!

        Murmurs of Leviathan he spoke,
        and rum was Plato in our heads. . .

"It's S.S. *Ala* — Antwerp — now remember kid
to put me out at three she sails on time.

33

I'm not much good at time any more keep
weakeyed watches sometimes snooze —" his bony hands
got to beating time. . . "A whaler once —
I ought to keep time and get over it — I'm a
Democrat — I know what time it is — No
I don't want to know what time it is — that
damned white Arctic killed my time. . ."

O Stamboul Rose — drums weave —

"I ran a donkey engine down there on the Canal
in Panama — got tired of that —
then Yucatan selling kitchenware — beads —
have you seen Popocatepetl — birdless mouth
with ashes sifting down — ?
                              and then the coast again. . ."

Rose of Stamboul O coral Queen —
teased remnants of the skeletons of cities —
and galleries, galleries of watergutted lava
snarling stone — green — drums — drown —

Sing!
" — that spiracle!" he shot a finger out the door. . .
"O life's a geyser — beautiful — my lungs —
No — I can't live on land — !"

I saw the frontiers gleaming of his mind;
or are there frontiers — running sands sometimes
running sands — somewhere — sands running. . .
Or they may start some white machine that sings.
Then you may laugh and dance the axletree —
steel — silver — kick the traces — and know —

ATLANTIS ROSE drums wreathe the rose,
the star floats burning in a gulf of tears
and sleep another thousand —

                              interminably
long since somebody's nickel — stopped —
playing —

A wind worried those wicker-neat lapels, the
swinging summer entrances to cooler hells...
Outside a wharf truck nearly ran him down
— he lunged up Bowery way while the dawn
was putting the Statue of Liberty out — that
torch of hers you know —

I started walking home across the Bridge...

     .   .   .   .

Blithe Yankee vanities, turreted sprites, winged
                              British repartees, skil-
ful savage sea-girls
that bloomed in the spring — Heave, weave
those bright designs the trade winds drive...

    Sweet opium and tea, Yo-ho!
     Pennies for porpoises that bank the keel!
     Fins whip the breeze around Japan!

Bright skysails ticketing the Line, wink round the Horn
to Frisco, Melbourne...
                              Pennants, parabolas —
clipper dreams indelible and ranging,
baronial white on lucky blue!

Perennial-*Cutty*-trophied-*Sark!*

Thermopylæ, Black Prince, Flying Cloud through Sunda
— scarfed of foam, their bellies veered green esplanades,
locked in wind-humors, ran their eastings down;

> *at Java Head freshened the nip*
> *(sweet opium and tea!)*
> *and turned and left us on the lee...*

Buntlines tusseling (91 days, 20 hours and anchored!)
                                                                Rainbow, Leander
(last trip a tragedy) — where can you be
Nimbus? and you rivals two —

> a long tack keeping —
>   *Taeping?*
>   *Ariel?*

IV

CAPE HATTERAS

The seas all crossed,
weathered the capes, the voyage done . . .
— WALT WHITMAN

⤤ CAPE HATTERAS

IMPONDERABLE the dinosaur
                sinks slow,
                        the mammoth saurian
                                ghoul, the eastern
                                        Cape. . .
While rises in the west the coastwise range,
                        slowly the hushed land —
Combustion at the astral core — the dorsal change
Of energy — convulsive shift of sand. . .
But we, who round the capes, the promontories
Where strange tongues vary messages of surf
Below grey citadels, repeating to the stars
The ancient names — return home to our own
Hearths, there to eat an apple and recall
The songs that gypsies dealt us at Marseille
Or how the priests walked — slowly through Bombay —
Or to read you, Walt,— knowing us in thrall

To that deep wonderment, our native clay
Whose depth of red, eternal flesh of Pocahontus —

Those continental folded aeons, surcharged
With sweetness below derricks, chimneys, tunnels —
Is veined by all that time has really pledged us. . .
And from above, thin squeaks of radio static,
The captured fume of space foams in our ears —
What whisperings of far watches on the main
Relapsing into silence, while time clears
Our lenses, lifts a focus, resurrects
A periscope to glimpse what joys or pain
Our eyes can share or answer — then deflects
Us, shunting to a labyrinth submersed
Where each sees only his dim past reversed. . .

But that star-glistered salver of infinity,
The circle, blind crucible of endless space,
Is sluiced by motion,— subjugated never.
Adam and Adam's answer in the forest
Left Hesperus mirrored in the lucid pool.
Now the eagle dominates our days, is jurist
Of the ambiguous cloud.   We know the strident rule
Of wings imperious. . . Space, instantaneous,
Flickers a moment, consumes us in its smile:
A flash over the horizon — shifting gears —
And we have laughter, or more sudden tears.
Dream cancels dream in this new realm of fact
From which we wake into the dream of act;
Seeing himself an atom in a shroud —
Man hears himself an engine in a cloud!

" — Recorders ages hence" — ah, syllables of faith!
Walt, tell me, Walt Whitman, if infinity

Be still the same as when you walked the beach
Near Paumanok — your lone patrol — and heard the wraith
Through surf, its bird note there a long time falling. . .
For you, the panoramas and this breed of towers,
Of you — the theme that's statured in the cliff.
O Saunterer on free ways still ahead!
Not this our empire yet, but labyrinth
Wherein your eyes, like the Great Navigator's without ship,
Gleam from the great stones of each prison crypt
Of canyoned traffic . . . Confronting the Exchange,
Surviving in a world of stocks,— they also range
Across the hills where second timber strays
Back over Connecticut farms, abandoned pastures,—
Sea eyes and tidal, undenying, bright with myth!

The nasal whine of power whips a new universe. . .
Where spouting pillars spoor the evening sky,
Under the looming stacks of the gigantic power house
Stars prick the eyes with sharp ammoniac proverbs,
New verities, new inklings in the velvet hummed
Of dynamos, where hearing's leash is strummed. . .
Power's script,— wound, bobbin-bound, refined —
Is stropped to the slap of belts on booming spools, spurred
Into the bulging bouillon, harnessed jelly of the stars.
Towards what? The forked crash of split thunder parts
Our hearing momentwise; but fast in whirling armatures,
As bright as frogs' eyes, giggling in the girth
Of steely gizzards — axle-bound, confined
In coiled precision, bunched in mutual glee
The bearings glint,— O murmurless and shined
In oilrinsed circles of blind ecstasy!

Stars scribble on our eyes the frosty sagas,
The gleaming cantos of unvanquished space. . .
O sinewy silver biplane, nudging the wind's withers!
There, from Kill Devils Hill at Kitty Hawk
Two brothers in their twinship left the dune;
Warping the gale, the Wright windwrestlers veered
Capeward, then blading the wind's flank, banked and spun
What ciphers risen from prophetic script,
What marathons new-set between the stars!
The soul, by naphtha fledged into new reaches
Already knows the closer clasp of Mars,—
New latitudes, unknotting, soon give place
To what fierce schedules, rife of doom apace!

Behold the dragon's covey — amphibian, ubiquitous
To hedge the seaboard, wrap the headland, ride
The blue's cloud-templed districts unto ether. . .
While Iliads glimmer through eyes raised in pride
Hell's belt springs wider into heaven's plumed side.
O bright circumferences, heights employed to fly
War's fiery kennel masked in downy offings,—
This tournament of space, the threshed and chiselled height,
Is baited by marauding circles, bludgeon flail
Of rancorous grenades whose screaming petals carve us
Wounds that we wrap with theorems sharp as hail!

Wheeled swiftly, wings emerge from larval-silver hangars.
Taut motors surge, space-gnawing, into flight;
Through sparkling visibility, outspread, unsleeping,
Wings clip the last peripheries of light. . .
Tellurian wind-sleuths on dawn patrol,

Each plane a hurtling javelin of winged ordnance,
Bristle the heights above a screeching gale to hover;
Surely no eye that Sunward Escadrille can cover!
There, meaningful, fledged as the Pleiades
With razor sheen they zoom each rapid helix!
Up-chartered choristers of their own speeding
They, cavalcade on escapade, shear Cumulus —
Lay siege and hurdle Cirrus down the skies!
While Cetus-like, O thou Dirigible, enormous Lounger
Of pendulous auroral beaches,— satellited wide
By convoy planes, moonferrets that rejoin thee
On fleeing balconies as thou dost glide,
— Hast splintered space!

                Low, shadowed of the Cape,
Regard the moving turrets! From grey decks
See scouting griffons rise through gaseous crepe
Hung low ... until a conch of thunder answers
Cloud-belfries, banging, while searchlights, like fencers,
Slit the sky's pancreas of foaming anthracite
Toward thee, O Corsair of the typhoon,— pilot, hear!
Thine eyes bicarbonated white by speed, O Skygak, see
How from thy path above the levin's lance
Thou sowest doom thou hast nor time nor chance
To reckon — as thy stilly eyes partake
What alcohol of space .. ! Remember, Falcon-Ace,
Thou hast there in thy wrist a Sanskrit charge
To conjugate infinity's dim marge —
Anew .. !

           But first, here at this height receive
The benediction of the shell's deep, sure reprieve!

Lead-perforated fuselage, escutcheoned wings
Lift agonized quittance, tilting from the invisible brink
Now eagle-bright, now

              quarry-hid, twist-

                      -ing, sink with

Enormous repercussive list-

                -ings down

Giddily spiralled

              gauntlets, upturned, unlooping

In guerrilla sleights, trapped in combustion gyr-
Ing, dance the curdled depth

                down whizzing

Zodiacs, dashed

        (now nearing fast the Cape!)

              down gravitation's

                vortex into crashed

. . . . dispersion . . . into mashed and shapeless debris. . . .
By Hatteras bunched the beached heap of high bravery!

    .   .   .   .   .

The stars have grooved our eyes with old persuasions
Of love and hatred, birth,— surcease of nations. . .
But who has held the heights more sure than thou,
O Walt! — Ascensions of thee hover in me now
As thou at junctions elegiac, there, of speed
With vast eternity, dost wield the rebound seed!
The competent loam, the probable grass,— travail
Of tides awash the pedestal of Everest, fail
Not less than thou in pure impulse inbred
To answer deepest soundings! O, upward from the dead

Thou bringest tally, and a pact, new bound
Of living brotherhood!

                    Thou, there beyond —
Glacial sierras and the flight of ravens,
Hermetically past condor zones, through zenith havens
Past where the albatross has offered up
His last wing-pulse, and downcast as a cup
That's drained, is shivered back to earth — thy wand
Has beat a song, O Walt,— there and beyond!
And this, thine other hand, upon my heart
Is plummet ushered of those tears that start
What memories of vigils, bloody, by that Cape,—
Ghoul-mound of man's perversity at balk
And fraternal massacre! Thou, pallid there as chalk
Hast kept of wounds, O Mourner, all that sum
That then from Appomattox stretched to Somme!

Cowslip and shad-blow, flaked like tethered foam
Around bared teeth of stallions, bloomed that spring
When first I read thy lines, rife as the loam
Of prairies, yet like breakers cliffward leaping!
O, early following thee, I searched the hill
Blue-writ and odor-firm with violets, 'til
With June the mountain laurel broke through green
And filled the forest with what clustrous sheen!
Potomac lilies,— then the Pontiac rose,
And Klondike edelweiss of occult snows!
White banks of moonlight came descending valleys —
How speechful on oak-vizored palisades,
As vibrantly I following down Sequoia alleys

Heard thunder's eloquence through green arcades
Set trumpets breathing in each clump and grass tuft — 'til
Gold autumn, captured, crowned the trembling hill!

Panis Angelicus! Eyes tranquil with the blaze
Of love's own diametric gaze, of love's amaze!
Not greatest, thou,— not first, nor last,— but near
And onward yielding past my utmost year.
Familiar, thou, as mendicants in public places;
Evasive — too — as dayspring's spreading arc to trace is:—
Our Meistersinger, thou set breath in steel;
And it was thou who on the boldest heel
Stood up and flung the span on even wing
Of that great Bridge, our Myth, whereof I sing!

Years of the Modern! Propulsions toward what capes?
But thou, *Panis Angelicus,* hast thou not seen
And passed that Barrier that none escapes —
But knows it leastwise as death-strife? — O, something green,
Beyond all sesames of science was thy choice
Wherewith to bind us throbbing with one voice,
New integers of Roman, Viking, Celt —
Thou, Vedic Caesar, to the greensward knelt!

And now, as launched in abysmal cupolas of space,
Toward endless terminals, Easters of speeding light —
Vast engines outward veering with seraphic grace
On clarion cylinders pass out of sight
To course that span of consciousness thou'st named
The Open Road — thy vision is reclaimed!
What heritage thou'st signalled to our hands!

And see! the rainbow's arch — how shimmeringly stands
Above the Cape's ghoul-mound, O joyous seer!
Recorders ages hence, yes, they shall hear
In their own veins uncancelled thy sure tread
And read thee by the aureole 'round thy head
Of pasture-shine, *Panis Angelicus!*

                              yes, Walt,

Afoot again, and onward without halt,—
Not soon, nor suddenly,— no, never to let go
   My hand
        in yours,
           Walt Whitman —
                so —

V

THREE SONGS

The one Sestos, the other Abydos hight.
— MARLOWE

SOUTHERN CROSS

I WANTED you, nameless Woman of the South,
No wraith, but utterly — as still more alone
The Southern Cross takes night
And lifts her girdles from her, one by one —
High, cool,
            wide from the slowly smoldering fire
Of lower heavens,—
                        vaporous scars!

Eve! Magdalene!
                or Mary, you?

Whatever call — falls vainly on the wave.
O simian Venus, homeless Eve,
Unwedded, stumbling gardenless to grieve
Windswept guitars on lonely decks forever;
Finally to answer all within one grave!

And this long wake of phosphor,
                        iridescent

Furrow of all our travel — trailed derision!
Eyes crumble at its kiss. Its long-drawn spell
Incites a yell. Slid on that backward vision
The mind is churned to spittle, whispering hell.

I wanted you ... The embers of the Cross
Climbed by aslant and huddling aromatically.
It is blood to remember; it is fire
To stammer back ... It is
God — your namelessness. And the wash —

All night the water combed you with black
Insolence. You crept out simmering, accomplished.
Water rattled that stinging coil, your
Rehearsed hair — docile, alas, from many arms.
Yes, Eve — wraith of my unloved seed!

The Cross, a phantom, buckled — dropped below the dawn.
Light drowned the lithic trillions of your spawn.

NATIONAL WINTER GARDEN

OUTSPOKEN buttocks in pink beads
Invite the necessary cloudy clinch
Of bandy eyes. . . . No extra mufflings here:
The world's one flagrant, sweating cinch.

And while legs waken salads in the brain
You pick your blonde out neatly through the smoke.
Always you wait for someone else though, always —
(Then rush the nearest exit through the smoke).

Always and last, before the final ring
When all the fireworks blare, begins
A tom-tom scrimmage with a somewhere violin,
Some cheapest echo of them all — begins.

And shall we call her whiter than the snow?
Sprayed first with ruby, then with emerald sheen —
Least tearful and least glad (who knows her smile?)
A caught slide shows her sandstone grey between.

Her eyes exist in swivellings of her teats,
Pearls whip her hips, a drench of whirling strands.
Her silly snake rings begin to mount, surmount
Each other — turquoise fakes on tinselled hands.

We wait that writhing pool, her pearls collapsed,
— All but her belly buried in the floor;
And the lewd trounce of a final muted beat!
We flee her spasm through a fleshless door. . . .

Yet, to the empty trapeze of your flesh,
O Magdalene, each comes back to die alone.
Then you, the burlesque of our lust — and faith,
Lug us back lifeward — bone by infant bone.

VIRGINIA

O RAIN at seven,
Pay-check at eleven —
Keep smiling the boss away,
Mary (what are you going to do?)
Gone seven — gone eleven,
And I'm still waiting you —

O blue-eyed Mary with the claret scarf,
    Saturday Mary, mine!

It's high carillon
From the popcorn bells!
Pigeons by the million —
And Spring in Prince Street
Where green figs gleam
By oyster shells!

O Mary, leaning from the high wheat tower,
    Let down your golden hair!

High in the noon of May
On cornices of daffodils
The slender violets stray.
Crap-shooting gangs in Bleecker reign,
Peonies with pony manes —
Forget-me-nots at windowpanes:

Out of the way-up nickel-dime tower shine,
  Cathedral Mary,
            shine! —

VI

QUAKER HILL

I see only the ideal. But no ideals
have ever been fully successful on
this earth.

—ISADORA DUNCAN

The gentian weaves her fringes,
The maple's loom is red.

—EMILY DICKINSON

QUAKER HILL

PERSPECTIVE never withers from their eyes;
They keep that docile edict of the Spring
That blends March with August Antarctic skies:
These are but cows that see no other thing
Than grass and snow, and their own inner being
Through the rich halo that they do not trouble
Even to cast upon the seasons fleeting
Though they should thin and die on last year's stubble.

And they are awkward, ponderous and uncoy . . .
While we who press the cider mill, regarding them —
We, who with pledges taste the bright annoy
Of friendship's acid wine, retarding phlegm,
Shifting reprisals ('til who shall tell us when
The jest is too sharp to be kindly?) boast
Much of our store of faith in other men
Who would, ourselves, stalk down the merriest ghost.

Above them old Mizzentop, palatial white
Hostelry — floor by floor to cinquefoil dormer

Portholes the ceilings stack their stoic height.
Long tiers of windows staring out toward former
Faces — loose panes crown the hill and gleam
At sunset with a silent, cobwebbed patience . . .
See them, like eyes that still uphold some dream
Through mapled vistas, cancelled reservations!

High from the central cupola, they say
One's glance could cross the borders of three states;
But I have seen death's stare in slow survey
From four horizons that no one relates . . .
Weekenders avid of their turf-won scores,
Here three hours from the semaphores, the Czars
Of golf, by twos and threes in plaid plusfours
Alight with sticks abristle and cigars.

This was the Promised Land, and still it is
To the persuasive suburban land agent
In bootleg roadhouses where the gin fizz
Bubbles in time to Hollywood's new love-nest pageant.
Fresh from the radio in the old Meeting House
(Now the New Avalon Hotel) volcanoes roar
A welcome to highsteppers that no mouse
Who saw the Friends there ever heard before.

What cunning neighbors history has in fine!
The woodlouse mortgages the ancient deal
Table that Powitzky buys for only nine-
Ty-five at Adams' auction,— eats the seal,
The spinster polish of antiquity . . .
Who holds the lease on time and on disgrace?

What eats the pattern with ubiquity?
Where are my kinsmen and the patriarch race?

The resigned factions of the dead preside.
Dead rangers bled their comfort on the snow;
But I must ask slain Iroquois to guide
Me farther than scalped Yankees knew to go:
Shoulder the curse of sundered parentage,
Wait for the postman driving from Birch Hill
With birthright by blackmail, the arrant page
That unfolds a new destiny to fill. . . .

So, must we from the hawk's far stemming view,
Must we descend as worm's eye to construe
Our love of all we touch, and take it to the Gate
As humbly as a guest who knows himself too late,
His news already told? Yes, while the heart is wrung,
Arise — yes, take this sheaf of dust upon your tongue!
In one last angelus lift throbbing throat —
Listen, transmuting silence with that stilly note

Of pain that Emily, that Isadora knew!
While high from dim elm-chancels hung with dew,
That triple-noted clause of moonlight —
Yes, whip-poor-will, unhusks the heart of fright,
Breaks us and saves, yes, breaks the heart, yet yields
That patience that is armour and that shields
Love from despair — when love foresees the end —
Leaf after autumnal leaf
                    break off,
                              descend —
                                        descend —

VII

THE TUNNEL

*To Find the Western path
Right thro' the Gates of Wrath.*
—BLAKE

THE TUNNEL

PERFORMANCES, assortments, résumés —
Up Times Square to Columbus Circle lights
Channel the congresses, nightly sessions,
Refractions of the thousand theatres, faces —
Mysterious kitchens. . . . You shall search them all.
Someday by heart you'll learn each famous sight
And watch the curtain lift in hell's despite;
You'll find the garden in the third act dead,
Finger your knees — and wish yourself in bed
With tabloid crime-sheets perched in easy sight.

> Then let you reach your hat
> and go.
> As usual, let you — also
> walking down — exclaim
> to twelve upward leaving
> a subscription praise
> for what time slays.

Or can't you quite make up your mind to ride;
A walk is better underneath the L a brisk

Ten blocks or so before? But you find yourself
Preparing penguin flexions of the arms,—
As usual you will meet the scuttle yawn:
The subway yawns the quickest promise home.

Be minimum, then, to swim the hiving swarms
Out of the Square, the Circle burning bright —
Avoid the glass doors gyring at your right,
Where boxed alone a second, eyes take fright
— Quite unprepared rush naked back to light:
And down beside the turnstile press the coin
Into the slot. The gongs already rattle.

> And so
> of cities you bespeak
> subways, rivered under streets
> and rivers. . . . In the car
> the overtone of motion
> underground, the monotone
> of motion is the sound
> of other faces, also underground —

"Let's have a pencil Jimmy — living now
at Floral Park
Flatbush — on the fourth of July —
like a pigeon's muddy dream — potatoes
to dig in the field — travlin the town — too —
night after night — the Culver line — the
girls all shaping up — it used to be —"

Our tongues recant like beaten weather vanes.
This answer lives like verdigris, like hair

Beyond extinction, surcease of the bone;
And repetition freezes — "What

"what do you want? getting weak on the links?
fandaddle daddy don't ask for change — IS THIS
FOURTEENTH? it's half past six she said — if
you don't like my gate why did you
swing on it, why *didja*
swing on it
anyhow — "

      And somehow anyhow swing —

The phonographs of hades in the brain
Are tunnels that re-wind themselves, and love
A burnt match skating in a urinal —
Somewhere above Fourteenth TAKE THE EXPRESS
To brush some new presentiment of pain —

"But I want service in this office SERVICE
I said — after
the show she cried a little afterwards but — "

Whose head is swinging from the swollen strap?
Whose body smokes along the bitten rails,
Bursts from a smoldering bundle far behind
In back forks of the chasms of the brain,—
Puffs from a riven stump far out behind
In interborough fissures of the mind . . . ?

And why do I often meet your visage here,
Your eyes like agate lanterns — on and on

Below the toothpaste and the dandruff ads?
— And did their riding eyes right through your side,
And did their eyes like unwashed platters ride?
And Death, aloft,— gigantically down
Probing through you — toward me, O evermore!
And when they dragged your retching flesh,
Your trembling hands that night through Baltimore —
That last night on the ballot rounds, did you
Shaking, did you deny the ticket, Poe?

For Gravesend Manor change at Chambers Street.
The platform hurries along to a dead stop.

The intent escalator lifts a serenade
Stilly
Of shoes, umbrellas, each eye attending its shoe, then
Bolting outright somewhere above where streets
Burst suddenly in rain. . . . The gongs recur:
Elbows and levers, guard and hissing door.
Thunder is galvothermic here below. . . . The car
Wheels off.   The train rounds, bending to a scream,
Taking the final level for the dive
Under the river —
And somewhat emptier than before,
Demented, for a hitching second, humps; then
Lets go. . . . Toward corners of the floor
Newspapers wing, revolve and wing.
Blank windows gargle signals through the roar.

And does the Dæmon take you home, also,
Wop washerwoman, with the bandaged hair?

THE TUNNEL

After the corridors are swept, the cuspidors —
The gaunt sky-barracks cleanly now, and bare,
O Genoese, do you bring mother eyes and hands
Back home to children and to golden hair?

Dæmon, demurring and eventful yawn!
Whose hideous laughter is a bellows mirth
— Or the muffled slaughter of a day in birth —
O cruelly to inoculate the brinking dawn
With antennæ toward worlds that glow and sink; —
To spoon us out more liquid than the dim
Locution of the eldest star, and pack
The conscience navelled in the plunging wind,
Umbilical to call — and straightway die!

O caught like pennies beneath soot and steam,
Kiss of our agony thou gatherest;
Condensed, thou takest all — shrill ganglia
Impassioned with some song we fail to keep.
And yet, like Lazarus, to feel the slope,
The sod and billow breaking,— lifting ground,
— A sound of waters bending astride the sky
Unceasing with some Word that will not die . . . !

    .   .   .   .   .

A tugboat, wheezing wreaths of steam,
Lunged past, with one galvanic blare stove up the River.
I counted the echoes assembling, one after one,
Searching, thumbing the midnight on the piers.
Lights, coasting, left the oily tympanum of waters;
The blackness somewhere gouged glass on a sky.

And this thy harbor, O my City, I have driven under,
Tossed from the coil of ticking towers. . . . Tomorrow,
And to be. . . . Here by the River that is East —
Here at the waters' edge the hands drop memory;
Shadowless in that abyss they unaccounting lie.
How far away the star has pooled the sea —
Or shall the hands be drawn away, to die?

Kiss of our agony Thou gatherest,
            O Hand of Fire
                        gatherest —

VIII

ATLANTIS

*Music is then the knowledge of that which
relates to love in harmony and system.*

— PLATO

✗ATLANTIS

THROUGH the bound cable strands, the arching path
Upward, veering with light, the flight of strings,—
Taut miles of shuttling moonlight syncopate
The whispered rush, telepathy of wires.
Up the index of night, granite and steel —
Transparent meshes — fleckless the gleaming staves —
 Sibylline voices flicker, waveringly stream
As though a god were issue of the strings. . . .

And through that cordage, threading with its call
One arc synoptic of all tides below —
Their labyrinthine mouths of history
Pouring reply as though all ships at sea
Complighted in one vibrant breath made cry,—
"Make thy love sure — to weave whose song we ply!"
— From black embankments, moveless soundings hailed,
So seven oceans answer from their dream.

And on, obliquely up bright carrier bars
New octaves trestle the twin monoliths

Beyond whose frosted capes the moon bequeaths
Two worlds of sleep (O arching strands of song!) —
Onward and up the crystal-flooded aisle
White tempest nets file upward, upward ring
With silver terraces the humming spars,
The loft of vision, palladium helm of stars.

Sheerly the eyes, like seagulls stung with rime —
Slit and propelled by glistening fins of light —
Pick biting way up towering looms that press
Sidelong with flight of blade on tendon blade
— Tomorrows into yesteryear — and link
What cipher-script of time no traveller reads
But who, through smoking pyres of love and death,
Searches the timeless laugh of mythic spears.

Like hails, farewells — up planet-sequined heights
Some trillion whispering hammers glimmer Tyre:
Serenely, sharply up the long anvil cry
Of inchling æons silence rivets Troy.
And you, aloft there — Jason! hesting Shout!
Still wrapping harness to the swarming air!
Silvery the rushing wake, surpassing call,
Beams yelling Æolus! splintered in the straits!

From gulfs unfolding, terrible of drums,
Tall Vision-of-the-Voyage, tensely spare —
Bridge, lifting night to cycloramic crest
Of deepest day — O Choir, translating time
Into what multitudinous Verb the suns
And synergy of waters ever fuse, recast

In myriad syllables,— Psalm of Cathay!
O Love, thy white, pervasive Paradigm . . . !

We left the haven hanging in the night —
Sheened harbor lanterns backward fled the keel.
Pacific here at time's end, bearing corn,—
Eyes stammer through the pangs of dust and steel.
And still the circular, indubitable frieze
Of heaven's meditation, yoking wave
To kneeling wave, one song devoutly binds —
The vernal strophe chimes from deathless strings!

O Thou steeled Cognizance whose leap commits
The agile precincts of the lark's return;
Within whose lariat sweep encinctured sing
In single chrysalis the many twain,—
Of stars Thou art the stitch and stallion glow
And like an organ, Thou, with sound of doom —
Sight, sound and flesh Thou leadest from time's realm
As love strikes clear direction for the helm.

Swift peal of secular light, intrinsic Myth
Whose fell unshadow is death's utter wound,—
O River-throated — iridescently upborne
Through the bright drench and fabric of our veins;
With white escarpments swinging into light,
Sustained in tears the cities are endowed
And justified conclamant with ripe fields
Revolving through their harvests in sweet torment.

Forever Deity's glittering Pledge, O Thou
Whose canticle fresh chemistry assigns

To wrapt inception and beatitude,—
Always through blinding cables, to our joy,
Of thy white seizure springs the prophecy:
Always through spiring cordage, pyramids
Of silver sequel, Deity's young name
Kinetic of white choiring wings . . . ascends.

Migrations that must needs void memory,
Inventions that cobblestone the heart,—
Unspeakable Thou Bridge to Thee, O Love.
Thy pardon for this history, whitest Flower,
O Answerer of all,— Anemone,—
Now while thy petals spend the suns about us, hold —
(O Thou whose radiance doth inherit me)
Atlantis,— hold thy floating singer late!

So to thine Everpresence, beyond time,
Like spears ensanguined of one tolling star
That bleeds infinity — the orphic strings,
Sidereal phalanxes, leap and converge:
— One Song, one Bridge of Fire! Is it Cathay,
Now pity steeps the grass and rainbows ring
The serpent with the eagle in the leaves . . . ?
Whispers antiphonal in azure swing.